Robert A Thompson

The Russian Settlement in California Known as Fort Ross

Founded 1812, abandoned 1841. Why the Russians came and why they
left.

Robert A Thompson

The Russian Settlement in California Known as Fort Ross
Founded 1812, abandoned 1841. Why the Russians came and why they left.

ISBN/EAN: 9783337169510

Printed in Europe, USA, Canada, Australia, Japan

Cover: Foto ©ninafisch / pixelio.de

More available books at **www.hansebooks.com**

RUSSIAN SETTLEMENT

in California.

Fort Ross, Sonoma County

By R. A. THOMPSON

SANTA ROSA, CAL.

1896

The

Russian Settlement

in

California

KNOWN AS FORT ROSS

Founded 1812 . . . Abandoned 1841

WHY THE RUSSIANS CAME AND WHY THEY LEFT

By R. A. Thompson

— · —

SANTA ROSA
SONOMA DEMOCRAT PUBLISHING COMPANY
1896

The Russians in California

CHAPTER I

The story of the rapid conquest of Siberia, beginning with the advance of Yermak, the robber chief, across the Ural mountains in the sixteenth century, ending with the discovery of the northwest coast of America by Admiral Behring of the Russian navy, is one of the most remarkable achievements in the conquest and occupation of a country in the annals of history.

Behring discovered the fur seal as well as the proximity of the Asiatic and American continents. In the course of time the rumors of the discoveries reached the European capitals of London and Madrid. It had a long way to travel overland to St. Petersburg. Once started, the rumors soon reached the sharp ears of the diplomatists and were promptly reported to their home governments.

The result was the fitting out of Captain Cook's expedition for discoveries in that quarter by the English, a like expedition from Mexico by order of the King of Spain.

In the English expedition came the first pioneers of American people to the Pacific coast: John Ledyard, a native of Connecticut, and Captain John Gore, a native of Virginia. The latter, on the death of Captain Cook at the Hawaiian islands, took command as the ranking officer, and returned with the fleet to England.

We omit the complications which arose between England and Spain over their respective claims on the northwest coast of America, the outgrowth of these early voyages, and return to the Russians, with whom we have directly to deal.

The charter of the Russian-American company gave them some extraordinary privileges, which, in fact, included the government of the country, and it soon absorbed all the various independent associations and became supreme on the northwest American coast.

A bold and enterprising adventurer named Shelekof, a man of great executive ability and energy, was mainly instrumental in organ-

izing the Russian-American Fur Company. He selected for the head of the monopoly he had created Alexander Baranoff. Baranoff was a striking type of the strong race from which he sprang. He started life as a clerk in a retail store in Moscow. This offered no field to a spirit so adventurous as his. He went to Siberia in 1780. He was actively engaged in business when Shelekof put him at the head of his company, and he never displayed better judgment than in this selection of an agent. Baranoff was energetic, daring, politic on occasion, and bold as Cæsar when boldness was needed. He could execute the plans of others, and with equal ability could conceive and execute plans of his own. His influence over the Russian was unlimited, and he ruled not only the natives but his more unruly countrymen of the lowest class who were sent out to him. He was a small man, under average in size, with blue eyes, a bald head and sallow complexion. He was diplomatic and could shape words for a flexible meaning, and when he wanted to could make them as direct as a rifle ball aimed pointblank. For instance, he wrote to his company "Send me a priest well-informed, who is a peaceable man, not suspicious and not biggotted." For the rest, he was in the habit of getting on periodical sprees on hot rum, in which he generally involved everybody around his

"castle" before he got through, but they never interfered with his business.

One of the most notable of the events of his life was the building out of American timber and the launching of the first American-built vessel on the northwest coast. It was named the Phœnix by Baranoff and was floated in August, 1794, and afterwards made regular trips between the American and Asiatic coast.

Starting about the same time, the Russians had crossed and occupied Siberia, had crossed Behring sea and occupied the American coast and established communication with Asia by a ship built of American timber, before the English moving on the Atlantic coast had yet more than reached the Mississippi river.

Nothing could better illustrate the push and drive of the people of this mighty nation now pressing, if it has not already attained, the first place among all European and Asiatic powers.

With this much by way of introduction, we will relate in detail the even more daring occupation by order of Baranoff of the territory of California, and it was undoubtedly his intention to hold it against its then owners for all time, and his successors would have done so but for the timely promulgation in 1823 of the Monroe Doctrine which gave notice to all the world that no occupation of American territory

by European powers would be tolerated by the United States.

This principle was finally and forever settled as far as Russia was concerned in its treaty with the United States of April 17, 1824, in which Russia agreed from thenceforth to establish no settlements on the American continent or any adjacent islands south of the parallel of 54.40. This treaty, though the Russian settlement in California was not mentioned, involved its abandonment and put an end to any further Russian encroachments in California.

The Russian American Fur Company had now concentrated all the fur interests of the northwest coast under the direction of Baranoff. They occupied all the Aleutian Islands and made a permanent settlement on the American coast. It was destined to play a large part in the history of California, as we shall see.

CHAPTER II.

The first event which may be considered as leading to the settlement of the Russians at Fort Ross, was the sailing from Sitka on March 8th, 1806, of Chamberlain Resanof, of the Russian-American Fur Company, on the ship Juno (formerly an American vessel) bound for California on a trading voyage. Before Resanof's return to Sitka he seems to have determined to make a settlement somewhere on the California coast where his company

could carry on agriculture, and trade with the Californians. It was deemed unnecessary to ask permission of Spain, as Spanish authority north of San Francisco Bay was not recognized by the Russians; and the Russian government had already authorized the company to extend Russian sovereignty as far south as possible without infringing on the rights of other nations.

Resanof was ambitious. He hoped to eventually acquire for his country all the territory from San Francisco Bay to the Columbia river. The important mission of locating the site for the future settlement was intrusted to Kuskof, who by order of Baranoff sailed on the Kodiak, and after touching at Trinidad, arrived at Bodega Bay (always called by the Russians Port Rumiantsoff) on January 8th, 1809. Here the Kodiak remained at anchor until August. After carefully exploring the surrounding country, some temporary buildings were erected, some otter and beaver skins were procured and friendly relations were established with the Indians.

On August 29th Kuskof sailed for Sitka, and upon his arrival was able to report favorably concerning the country. He had found a fine climate, good tillable lands, plenty of fish and fur-bearing animals and a tolerable harbor. And as the country was entirely unoccupied by European or American settlers, the conditions were favorable for the

colony. So the Czar of Russia was petitioned to open negotiations with Spain with a view of a treaty allowing trade with New Albion, as Northern California was then called. And he was also asked to give the settlement the protection of the Russian government in case of opposition by the Americans. And this protection, it is said, was promised by the Czar; while, as to trading with the Californians, the company were told to make such terms as they could. Upon receiving this encouragement, Kuskof attempted a new expedition to Bodega, but was unsuccessful, for while stopping at Queen Charlotte's island, he was attacked by Indians and was compelled to return to Sitka.

In 1811, Kuskof again sailed for Bodega in the schooner Chirikof and upon his arrival he at once renewed his explorations in the endeavor if possible to find a better place than Bodega at which to establish his headquarters and build his fort. He found a place, sixteen miles by water north of Bodega, called by the Indians Madshui-nui where, though there was no land-locked bay, there was excellent anchorage, and good protection from all summer winds; and he found that all other advantages, such as soil, timber, water and pasturage were much better than at Bodega.

The valley of the Slavianka (Russian River) was examined for fifty miles but no place was found that compared favorably with Mad-shui-mui, so after a thorough investigation of the whole country, Mad-shui-mui was chosen and work was commenced at once. The site selected was a table-land about 100 feet above the ocean and containing something over 1000 acres land was according to Russian observation in latitude 38' 33' longitude 123 15' (our coast pilot puts it now in lat. 38° 30' long. 123' 15'). The friendship of the native chiefs was secured by making them presents and the Russians claim, and it is probably true, that the country was ceded by the Indians to the Company There were at this time in the Russian Colony, 95 Russians, including 25 mechanics. There were also about 80 Aleuts with a fleet of 40 bidarkas (skin boats). The Aleuts were sent out to hunt otter along the coast, but with instructions to not enter San Francisco Bay, for it was oest at this time not to offend the Spaniards. The Russians prepared timber for several months and when all was ready the Aleuts were recalled to aid the mechanics, and all went to work on the fort and other necessary buildings. And in a few months a fortified village had arisen on the shore of New Albion. In the fort were mounted at first only twelve cannon, but the number of cannon was increased to about forty in after years. All was completed early in September and

on September 10th, or August 30th of the Russian calendar, the name day of Emperor Alexander, the establishment was formally dedicated with great festivity and named Ross from the root of the name Russia, a word extending far back into antiquity.

As to the exact original meaning of the word Ross there seems to be a difference of opinion, but it is certain that the people of the Volga were formerly called Rus, and the Russians generally were called the people of Ross, and the country is yet called Rossia or Russia.

About this time there was distributed over California a proclamation issued by the Russian American Fur Company and addressed to the people of California. It was a very conciliatory document and was intended to make friends of the Californians, and thus advance the interests of the Russians. But it seems to have done no good, for the Californians were jealous of their own rights and suspicious of foreigners. Thus it was that the Russians, in less than a year's time, found themselves firmly planted in California without having met with any resistance from the Indians or Spaniards. The Spanish were cognizant of what was going on at Ross, but were entirely unable to prevent it. But in August, just before the dedication of Ross, Commandanet Arguello, of San Francisco, sent Moraga, "a Spanish officer," with seven men, to

Ross to investigate. Moraga returned September 1st and reported that the Russians had built a fort protected by artillery, and apparently intended to remain. Moraga was courteously received by the Russians and was allowed to make a complete inspection of the fort.

Morago was again sent to Ross, in January, 1813, when he conferred with Kuskof about trade. He was made acquainted with the plans of the strangers and returned January 27th. Arguello communicated to the Viceroy the result of Morago's two visits to Ross. There is nothing in the Spanish record to show that the Governor or Commandante of California ever gave the Russians permission to settle in the country or even consented to trade with them without the Viceroy's permission. Meantime, the Viceroy had learned that the Russians had settled on the coast, and in July he wrote to Arriaga instructing him to watch the strangers. He did not fear hostilities from the Russians, but feared that they were not what they seemed. They might be connected with Anglo-American designs upon California. Three weeks later, on receipt of Arriaga's letter, the Viceroy again wrote, enclosing the treaty between Russia and Spain, and instructing the Commandante to notify Kuskof that his occupation of Californian territory was a clear violation of the treaty, and requesting him to immediately remove his establishment.

CHAPTER III.

Meanwhile the Russians were to be closely watched, and the military authorities of the peninsula and also of the interior were to hold themselves in readiness to furnish aid in case of an emergency. These communications reached California early in 1814, and in April Moraga was a third time sent with an escort to Ross with letters in which Arriaga made known to Kuskof the Viceroy's instructions. The Russian commander declined to give a definite answer until he could hear from his superior, Baranoff. So he waited until June before answering, and then he answered, that as he did not fully understand the Spanish letters, he could not act officially upon them. These letters were carried to San Francisco by the agent, Slobodchikof, who took down a small cargo of goods to trade for grain. The Russians hoped that the trouble caused by the Viceroy's orders would blow over, so that trade might proceed. It was the company's policy to keep affairs as quiet as possible at St. Petersburg and Madrid, and to trust for the permanence and prosperity of Ross to the revolutionary condition and consequent weakness of Mexico. On July 30th Moraga made out a full report on the establishment of Ross, particularly on the strength of its defenses.

In 1815 Arguello wrote a peremptory letter to Kuskof, stating that by the Viceroy's orders, the settlement at Ross must be immediately abandoned, if friendly relations were to be maintained between Russia and Spain. Kuskof's reply was that he could do nothing without instructions from his superior, Baranof. Yet in August the Russian vessel Suvarof, Captain Makarof, arrived at San Francisco and trade continued. In 1816 there arrived at San Francisco a Russian vessel, the Rurick, with a scientific expedition, under command of Lieutenant Otto Von Kotzebue, and Sola came up from Monterey and made a complaint concerning the actions of the Russians at Ross. Kotzebue said he had no authority to act, but consented to send for Kuskof. The latter went to San Francisco and a consultation was held at the Presidio, but nothing came of it, as Kuskof would do nothing. And as the Spaniards knew that Ross was impregnable to any force that the Californians could bring against it, the Russians were not interfered with.

The following is a description of the settlement as it appeared at this time: The site of the fort, eight miles northwest of the mouth of Russian river, is about 150 yards from the sea, on a plateau 100 feet above the water, and is so protected by ravines as to be of difficult access to an enemy. All the buildings are of redwood. The fort is a quadrangular enclosure of about 300 by 250 feet, its angles facing the Cardinal points. It is formed

of heavy timbers eight inches thick and fifteen feet long set upright and buried three feet in the ground, leaving them twelve feet high and surmounted by a horizontal beam or plate, on which are spiked thinner timbers, three feet long and sharpened at the top. On the north corner of this inclosure is a heptagon blockhouse watch tower, solidly built of timbers one foot thick. It is twenty-five feet in diameter and two stories high and has fourteen port-holes for cannon. On the south corner is an octagon blockhouse watch-tower, twenty-eight feet in diameter and with sixteen port-holes for cannon. There are also some twenty port-holes in the stockade. All of these port-holes when not in use are closed by a block of wood hung on heavy wrought-iron hand-made hinges, this stopper being of the same thickness as the wall and fastened on the inside by a heavy iron bar. On the east corner, and just inside of the stockade is the chapel, twenty-five by thirty feet and surmounted by a belfry with a chime of bells, and a dome. Within the fort are the Commandante's house, the officers' quarters, barracks for the Russian employes and various storehouses and domestic offices. Some of the buildings are of two stories. The commandante's house has glass windows, carpets and a piano. The chapel is decorated with paintings and all present a neat appearance. A well in the inclosure supplied water for emergencies but a well outside and the creek furnished water for ordinary uses. Outside the stockade are the huts of the Aleuts and natives and in the immediate neighborhood is a windmill for grinding grain, a tannery, workshops, farm buildings, granaries, cattle-yards, etc. Beyond is the vegetable garden, and down at the foot of the cliff is a small wharf and boat-landing. Near by is a shed for the protection of the bidarkas or skin-boats, another shed for storing lumber, another for work connected with the building of vessels, a blacksmith shop and a bath house. At Bodega there are some warehouses and at the half-way house near the river there is a station occupied like that at Bodega by some servants of the company. The population of Ross averaged from 200 to 400. The Russians were officers, chiefs of hunting parties, and mechanics. The Aleuts were hunters and fishermen. The California Indians were laborers and servants. All were, when necessary, farmers and soldiers. From 1812 to 1840 the Russians kept up an establishment at the Farallones as well as at Ross. The object was to capture fur seals, 1200 to 1500 skins being taken annually though Winship, Gale, Smith and other Americans had taken the cream of this wealth a few years earlier. After 1818 the seals diminished rapidly until only about 500 could be caught annually. Still the Rus-

sians kept five or six Aleuts at the Islands to kill sea-lions and gulls and gather eggs for use at Ross and Sitka. Annually about from 5000 to 50,000 gulls and about 200 sea-lions were killed. Of the latter, the meat was salted for use, the skins were used for making boats and the bladders were made into watertight sacks, and the blubber was tried out for oil, both as food and for lamps, as the hunt for otter became less and less profitable. And as obstacles interfered with success in the way of trade, the agents of the company turned their attention more and more to home industries at Ross. Agriculture was naturally one of the most important of these industries. A considerable quantity of dried beef, leather and butter was sent to Sitka after the home wants were supplied and at last the company had 2000 cattle, 1000 horses and 1000 sheep to sell with the establishment. The first livestock was obtained from the Californians, but not without difficulty, as trade was prohibited. There was scarcely any article of wood, iron or leather which the mechanics of Ross could not make of a quality sufficiently good for the California market, and to the very last they received frequent applications from the Spaniards. Several boats were built for the Spanish officers or friars. Timber and tiles were sent north and south and even to the Sandwich Islands. Pine pitch was sent in large quantities to Sitka in barrels, which, like those used for butter and meat, were made at Ross. Four vessels of respectable dimensions were built at Ross before 1824 and three of them, the Ruldakof, Volga and the Kiakta, the reader meets in southern ports.

CHAPTER IV.

In 1821 Kuskof died and was succeeded in command by Karl Schmidt. Schmidt died in 1823, In 1828 Duhant Cilley, a Frenchman who was making a tour around the world in his yacht, arrived at Ross. He made a sketch of the place as he found it. He reported finding here all the luxuries used in Europe but unknown in other parts of California. He gave a detailed description of the orchard and the fence around it, etc.

Vessels continued to arrive at San Francisco, two or three a year, from Ross and Sitka, with goods to trade for grain and other articles which could be procured from the Spaniards. In 1831 the Russians made an attempt to extend their agricultural possessions south-easterly but they desisted on account of the strong opposition of the Californians. In 1832 Governor Figuroa was instructed to report in detail on the force maintained by the Russians and the probable intentions of the strangers. He was also ordered to establish settlements in the north to check farther encroachments. In 1833, Figuroa sent Al-

feres Vallejo to Ross to purchase arms, munitions and clothing for the Californian soldiers and at the same time to secretly acquaint himself with the exact condition of affairs. Vallejo carried letters to manager Kostromitinoff and to Wrangell whom it was thought might have arrived. These letters were filled with expressions of friendship and good-will and of a desire for closer friendship and commerce with those highly es-

trampled upon the laws of nations and aimed at territorial encroachment. Wrangell was expected at Ross to found a new settlement at Santa Rosa, and with the same object in view the desertion of the neophytes of San Rafael was being encouraged.

Wrangell finally arrived at Ross and employed Hartnell as an agent to obtain cargoes of produce and if possible to secure certain concessions in regard to the payment of

Fort Ross in 1828, from a sketch by Duhaut Cilley.

teemed neighbors, the Russians. The manager of Ross was also urged to use his influence with the Czar to promote the recognition of Mexican independence. Vallejo succeeded in purchasing the required articles at Ross and on March 5th made his report.

Two days later Figuroa wrote to the national government at Mexico denouncing those highly esteemed neighbors as intruders who had

duties. Wrangell also wrote to Figuroa a letter in which he warmly defended his country against the charges of the English navigator, Beechey, charges which he declared to be without foundation to the effect that Russians had grievously wronged the Californians by killing otter illegally, by engaging in contraband trade, and even taking possession of the Santa Barbara islands. Other foreigners had

certainly done these things, but the Russians never.

In 1836 manager Kostromitinoff was succeeded by Alexander Rotchef. The ex-manager seems to have succeeded Hartnell as agent of the company at San Francisco. He obtained from the Governor of California a permission to erect a warehouse for his company on any site which he might select. With Captain Richardson's consent he decided to build at Sausalito. But before any use was made of this concession the deputation took up the matter and decided that the governor had no power to grant such a privilege, and that it was not expedient to allow a foreign company to secure such a foothold in a Mexican port. Accordingly, in September, Gutierres issued an order that no building should be erected. Subsequently, in 1839, Rotchef petitioned for the privilege of building a warehouse at Yerba Buena, but the concession was not granted.

During this period Sonoma was founded as a pueblo; and several citizens, chiefly foreigners, were permitted to occupy ranchos on the northern frontier, all with a view to check the apprehended advance of the Russians.

Again, in 1839, Vallejo warned the Mexican government of danger from the Russians which might be averted only by an increase of the force at Sonoma.

In 1837 Ross was visited by Slocum and in 1839 by Laplace, each of whom published a description of the place. Meanwhile Governor Wrangell was very anxious to acquire more territory to the south and east of Ross. He wished to extend his possessions at least to San Francisco Bay on the south and to Sacramento on the east, and if this was to be done it must be done at once, as the most favorable time had already passed. If this territory should be occupied against the wishes of the Californians it would not only anger them but would be sure to meet with strong opposition from foreign powers. So Wrangell's best plan was to conciliate the Californians. He wished to present farther and in a stronger light, as the Russians had been doing for years, the danger of encroachment by other foreigners, especially the Americans. Also the marked contrast between the past conduct of his people and those of other nations, and the manifest advantage of preferring such friendly and orderly neighbors, rather than the horde of turbulent adventurers who were sure to get possession of the northern frontier.

Wrangell wished to go to Mexico in person to secure from the authorities of the republic at once a cession or sale of the desired territory. The company having approved his plan and agreed to pay for the establishments of San Rafael and Sonoma, in case Mexico would consent to cede the territory, the Baron resigned his position as Governor

of the American Colonies and obtained permission to return to Russia by way of Mexico, with authority to represent the Colonial Government in negotiations with the Republic of Mexico. With his instructions came a successor to Wrangell in the person of Ivan Ruprianof and the ex-governor sailed at once. After his arrival at Mexico he with some difficulty obtained an interview with Vice-President Barragan and other high officials, but he could accomplish nothing, as the Mexicans would not entertain the proposition to cede any territory on any terms.

CHAPTER V.

With the failure of Wrangell's mission the company decided to abandon Ross, and they at once began to seek a purchaser. At a conference between Ruprianof and Douglas of the Hudson Bay Company, a proposition was made to sell Ross for $30,000. "Of course," writes Douglas in his journal, "they cannot sell the soil but merely the improvements, which we can only hold through a native." An answer was to be given in the autumn after a consultation with McLaughlin. But the English company decided that the purchase was not desirable as it would very likely displease the Californians and would probably cause serious complications with the United States.

This negotiation having failed, the company next tried Alverado.

The governor asked for farther information as to the nature of the property offered and made haste to inform the Mexican government of the impending change and a long correspondence ensued, but no trade resulted. The American ship, Lausanne, Captain Josiah Spaulding, coming down from Columbia in July, 1840, believing Bodega to be a free port, belonging to Russia, thought he might land his passengers there and perhaps accomplish something in the way of trade without paying anchorage dues or other duties. The Russians had never before permitted such operations and on this occasion it seems that Rotchef told Spaulding that he must not trade nor go by land to San Francisco as he had intended But Rotchef then went to Monterey, leaving the Lausanne at Bodega, and the captain, crew and passengers were free to do as they pleased as there was no Russian guard nearer than Ross. So Spaulding also started for San Francisco with McIntosh as a guide. Four of the passengers went to Sonoma to ask Vallejo for pass-ports which should enable them to remain in the country. Vallejo was naturally startled at the appearance of the armed foreigners, with the news that Bodega was practically abandoned by the Russians and that a foreign vessel was lying there free from all restrictions in respect of contraband trade or of landing passengers. He immediately despatched Alferes

Lazaro Pina and a guard of soldiers to Bodega with instructions to re-embark all persons who had landed and to enjoin upon those in charge of the vessel to land no goods on penalty of being treated as smugglers. As Monterey was the only port open to foreign trade, Pina was to remain at his post, prevent all traffic and intercourse, keep a strict watch and report. Subsequently he was directed to collect tonnage dues on the Lausanne at the rate of $1.50 per ton. Spaulding, accompanied by several persons from San Francisco who were traveling without passports, called at Sonoma on his way to Bodega. His companions were not allowed to proceed and the captain was called upon to pay his tonnage dues. He declined to do so on the ground that Bodega was a free port belonging to Russia; but after discussion he agreed to pay the demand if it should be declared lawful by the proper authorities. He was then allowed to depart with an order to Pina to return to Sonoma as soon as the vessel had sailed. As Spaulding had cited the manager at Ross in confirmation of his claim that Bodega was a Russian port, Vallejo instructed Pina to state clearly to Rotchef that Bodega belonged to Mexico and not to Russia though the use of it by Russian vessels had been tolerated. That the commander at Ross had no control of it, except by permission of the Californian government, that he had no right to find it

strange that Californian troops were stationed there, especially when he was in the habit of traveling in the country without a permit and in disrespect of the frontier authorities; and of representing to visitors that Bodega was a free port, and of taking the liberty to permit foreigners to enter the country in defiance of law. Meanwhile Rotchef came back from Monterey and was filled with wrath when he found the soldiers on guard and saw a copy made by a subordinate, in his absence, of Vallejo's instructions to Pina. He was violent and insulting in his anger. He raised the Russian flag, defying the Californians to pull it down, and offered his protection to the foreign passengers who went with him to Ross. Pina made no resistance, but reported to Vallejo. The latter sent a communication on the matter to Rotchef and another to be forwarded to the Governor at Sitka. But Rotchef refused to receive the documents. Vallejo subsequently issued an order forbidding Rotchef or any of his men to travel in the country without a license. The Lausanne sailed away about July 26th, leaving five or six foreigners who were aided by the Russians to reach Sacramento. Pina by Vallejo's order did not attempt to interfere beyond warning Rotchef that he would be held responsible for the entrance of the men. Much more angry correspondence followed, but it is not important at this late day.

In January, 1841, Vallejo reported to the minister of war concerning his controversy with Rotchef. He took much credit to himself and mentioned as a result of that controversy, the proposed abandonment of Ross. The Russians had consulted him as to their right to sell to a private person the buildings as well as the live-stock, and he had told them that the nation had the first right and must be consulted. The reason why this cautious answer was given was that some foreigners from the Columbia or elsewhere might outbid a citizen of California and thus raise a question of sovereignty which might prove troublesome to the Mexican interests in the future.

Vallejo also urged the government to furnish a garrison and authorize the planting of a colony at Ross upon its abandonment by the Russians. In February, Kostromitinoff, representing the company, offered to sell the property to Vallejo himself for $30,000, payable half in cash or in bills of the Hudson Bay Company and half in produce delivered at Yerba Buena. The general was willing to entertain the proposition but could not make a definite answer until July or August, as he must have authority from his government. When the answer came from Mexico it was not a satisfactory one, as the Mexican government seemed to think that the Russians had been frightened away and would leave a flourishing settlement to be taken possession of by the Californians as soon as they were gone. So Vallejo received some useless instructions about the details of the occupation and the form of government to be established at Ross.

In July, Kostromitinoff, having returned from Sitka, an elaborate inventory was made of the property offered. Vallejo and Alverado were again approached but they absolutely declined to purchase, as they had concluded that the property should and would revert to the Californians and that no other purchaser could be found. Alverado stated in a letter that his only fear was that the Russians would burn the buildings rather than let them fall into the hands of the Californians. But there was another purchaser, John A. Sutter. The bargain was made in September. The formal contract was signed by Kostromitinoff and Sutter in the office of the Subprefect at San Francisco, with Voiget and Leese as witnesses, on December 13, 1840.

CHAPTER VI.

By the terms of the contract Sutter was to pay for the property specified in the inventory, $30,000, payable in installments. The establishment at New Helvetia (Sacramento) and the property at Bodega, and the two ranches of Khlebnikof and Tschernich, "which property was to be left intact in possession of the company's agents,"

were pledged as guarantees for the payment. The Russians say that the contract was approved by the California government and it is certain that no official disapproval was made.

Sutter obtained from manager Rotchef a certificate of transfer of the land, dated one day earlier than the contract, in which document the commander certified that the company had held peaceable possession for 29 years and that they had sold it to M. Le Capitaine Sutter for $30,000 and had delivered it into his possession indisputably. This document in after years was paraded as Sutter's Deed and was made the basis of a somewhat plausible claim to the possession of the land. Manager Rotchef with all the remaining servants of the company sailed on the Constantine which left San Francisco in December, 1841, and probably left Ross in January, 1842. A few Russians remained on the ranchos to look after the company's interest. Sutter sent Roberts to look out for him at first, but John Bidwell took his place early in 1842. He was succeeded by Wm. Benitz in 1843.

In the meantime most of the movable property and live-stock were removed to New Helvetia. A few hundred cattle were left, as they were too wild to be driven. The Californians made no effort to occupy the place, for as they had virtually consented to the sale the State had nothing at Ross to pro-tect. In 1845 the Mexican government granted to Manuel Torres four leagues of land called the Muniz grant, including the establishment of Ross. Torres sold the grant to Wm. Benitz, and Benitz, afterwards, to avoid a law-suit, also bought for 6,000 dollars the Sutter or Russian title.

The inventory by which the property was sold to Sutter includes the following: A square fort of logs 1088 feet in circumference, twelve feet high with two watch-towers, a house of squared logs, 36 by 58 feet, double board roof, six rooms with corridor and kitchen. Another block house 24 by 48 feet with six rooms and corridor. House for revenue officers, 22 by 60 feet, ten rooms; barracks 24 by 66 feet, eight rooms; three warehouses, kitchen, jail, chapel with a belfry and dome. Outside of the fort, blacksmith-shop, tannery, boat-house, cooper's shop, bakery, carpenter's shop, two wind-mills for grinding, one mill moved by animal power, three threshing floors, a well, stable, sheep-cote, dairy-house, two cow stables, hog-pen, corral, ten sheds, eight baths, ten kitchens, 24 houses, nearly every one having an orchard. At Kostromitinoff rancho, house, farm buildings, corral and boat for cross-ing the river Slavianka (Russian); at Khebnikof rancho, adobe house, farm buildings, bath, well, corral. At Jorges rancho (Russian Gulch), house, stores, fences, etc. At Bodega, warehouse 30 by 60 feet; three

small houses, bath, ovens and corrals.

The purchase also included the schooner Constantine, which was rechristened the Sacramento. This vessel made frequent trips between Ross, Bodega and Sacramento, taking from Ross to Sacramento all the movable property bought by Sutter which could be utilized. Even several of the newest houses were taken down and moved. The one cannon left at Ross was taken to Sacramento and was finally donated by Sutter to the California pioneers. About 4,000 head of cattle, horses and sheep were driven overland, and one old Indian who assisted in the driving is still to be seen occasionally at Ross. Ross, as it was called by the Russians, was always called by the Spaniards El Fuerte de Los Rusos or Fuerte Ruso, and by the Americans who afterwards settled in California Fort Ross, and as this old settlement is a place of much interest and is annually visited by hundreds of people from all parts of the country, it may be interesting to give a brief account of it as it is at present, 1896.

The property is now owned by G. W. Call, who does what he can to preserve the old buildings and does carefully keep all old relics which are not perishable. The chapel stands perfectly erect with the original roof, doors and windows intact. During all these 83 years the little belfry and dome have stood bravely facing the heavy winter storms. The stockade is mostly gone, as the timbers were not selected but were evidently made of young timber with sap on. The watch towers are badly decayed on the southerly or storm side but are sound on the north side. The governor's house is in a good state of preservation because it has had a new roof and has been weatherboarded outside. It is now used as a hotel. The barracks building is in a fair state of preservation. These old buildings, with half-a-dozen new buildings, a wharf and a chute at the landing and two dairies constitute the present settlement of Fort Ross. One millstone made from native stone remains intact. Of the original apple-trees some 50 are still alive and bear apples every year. A portion of the original fence still stands and does duty just as it did when described by Duhant Cilley in 1828. A painting copied from the sketch made by Cilley has also been preserved and in the hotel may still be seen in service an old piano made by Bord in Paris about 1820. In a little valley where the Russians cut away all the trees has grown a forest of redwood and pine trees, some of them over five feet in diameter. The pines have evidently grown from seed, but all the redwoods are sprouts sprung from the stumps of the trees cut down. This second-growth forest proves conclusively that all the

Californians have to do to perpetuate the redwood forests is to give them a chance. The Russian bishop, Vladimir. a few years ago, visited Fort Ross and made a proposition to purchase the old chapel, with a few acres of ground, including the Russian cemetery, with a view of preserving them. But as Vladimir was recalled the negotiation was not consummated.

CHAPTER VII.

We have given in the preceding chapters a consecutive and concise history of the Russian settlement at Ross. Some contemporary accounts of this interesting event which have appeared from time to time written by those who described their visits to the settlement will now be given.

Among the most interesting accounts of Ross is that of Sir George Simpson, governor-in-chief of the Hudson Bay Company, who came to California in 1841, and afterwards published a most interesting narrative of his voyage.

Governor Simpson evidently came to California with the view of seeing if there was any way of acquiring possession of the country for the English government. He visited General Vallejo at Sonoma and received no encouragement from that true and loyal friend of the United States. However, he gives a very sprightly account of his visit and we reproduce that portion which refers to Ross. On approaching the coast of California the governor says:

"In the course of the morning, we passed Bodega and Ross, respectively the harbor and the fort of the Russian American Company. That association, which assumed its present form towards the close of the last century, under the patronage of the Emperor Paul, could not find any native supply of bread-stuffs nearer than the central steppes of Asia, to be transported thence over about a hundred and twenty degrees of longitude and thirty of latitude, by barges from the head of the Sena to Yakutsk, on horses from Yakutsk to Ochotsk, and in ships from Ochotsk to Sitka. So expensive and tedious a route operating almost as a prohibition, the Company's establishments were, of course, very inadequately supplied with that which, to a Russian, is peculiarly the staff of life, so that a design was naturally formed of planting an agricultural settlement on the adjacent coast of America.

"With this view, in March, 1806, —the very month, by the by, in which Lewis and Clarke left their winter's encampment of Clatsop Point to retrace their steps across the continent—Von Resanoff, who was then the Company's principal representative, attempted to enter the Columbia, but was baffled in the attempt by the same circumstances which had so long retarded the discovery of the river. Eight

years afterwards, however, the extensive and beautiful valley of Santa Rosa, which opens into Bodega Bay, was actually occupied —Spain being too busy elsewhere with more serious evils to repel the intrusion.

As compared with the Columbia, California, besides its great fertility and its easier access, possessed the sea-otters, besides a large supply of fur-seals, having thereby so far diminished the breeds as to throw nearly all the expense of their establishments on the agricultural branch of the business—an expense far exceeding the mere cost of production, with a reasonable freight. The Californian settlement required ships exclusively for itself; and,

Fort Ross in 1940, looking northeast from bluff.

additional recommendation of literally teeming with sea-otters, thus securing to the Company an incidental advantage, more important, perhaps, in a pecuniary sense, than the primary object of pursuit. Since 1814, the Russians have sent to market from California the enormous number of eighty thousand though the Russians had so far conciliated the local authorities as to be permitted to hunt both on the coast and in the interior, they were yet obliged, by the undisguised jealousy and dislike of their presence, constantly to maintain a military attitude, with strong fortifications and considerable garrisons.

Kodiak Indian Skin Boat used at Ross.

"That the Russians ever actually intended to claim the sovereignty of this part of the coast, I do not believe. The term Ross was certainly suspicious, as being the constant appellation of the ever-varying phases of Russia from the days of Ruric, the very name under which, nearly ten centuries ago, the red-bearded dwellers on the Borysthenes, who have since spread themselves with resistless pertinacity over more than two hundred degrees of longitude, carried terror and desolation in their crazy boats to the gates of Constantinople, a city destined alike to be their earliest quarry and their latest prey. So expansive a monosyllable could hardly be a welcome neighbor to powers so feeble and jealous as Spain and Mexico.

"In justice, however, to Russia, I have no hesitation in saying that, under the recognized principles of colonization, she is fully entitled to all that she holds in America. As early as 1741, Beering and Tschirikoff had visited the continent respectively in 59° and 56°, about a degree above Sitka, and about a degree below it—the former, moreover, seeing many islands, and perhaps the peninsula of Alaska, on his return; and, by the year 1763, private adventurers had explored the whole width of the ocean, discovering the intermediate chain of islands, from the scene of Beering's shipwreck, in the vicinity of Kamschatka, to Alaska, then erroneous-ly supposed to be an island, and thence still further eastward to Kodyak—no other nation having previously penetrated, or even pretended to have penetrated, farther north than the parallel of fifty-three degrees.

"But the Russian discoveries were distinguished by this favorable peculiarity, that they were, in a great measure, achieved independently of the more southerly discoveries of Spain, being the result of rumors of a neighboring continent, which, in the beginning of the century, the Russian conquerors had found to be rife in Kamschatka. Moreover, in the case of the Russians, discovery and possession had advanced hand in hand. The settlement of Kodyak was formed four years before Meares erected his solitary shed in Nootka Sound; and Sitka was established fully ten or twelve years earlier than Astoria."

Governor Simpson says on page 283, vol. 1, of his interesting work:

"On emerging from the strait, which is about three miles long, we saw on our left, in a deep bay, known as Whalers' Harbor, two vessels,— the Government schooner California and the Russian brig Constantine, now bound to Sitka, with the last of the tenants of Bodega and Ross on board. As we observed the Russians getting under way, I despatched Mr. Hopkins in one of our boats, in order to express my regret at being thus

deprived of the anticipated pleasure of paying my respects in person.

"Mr. Hopkins found about a hundred souls, men, women and children, all patriotically delighted to exchange the lovely climate of California for the ungenial skies of Sitka, and that too at the expense of making a long voyage in an old, crazy, clumsy tub, at the stormiest season of the year; but to this general rule there had been one exception, inasmuch as they had lost two days in waiting—but, alas! in vain—for a young woman, who had abjured alike her country and her husband for the sake of one of the dons of San Francisco.]

"Mr. Hopkins farther learned that, though it was Thursday with us, yet it was Friday with our northern friends; a circumstance which, besides showing that the Russians had not the superstition of our tars as to days of sailing, forcibly reminded us that between them the two parties had passed round the globe in opposite directions to prosecute one and the same trade in furs, which the indolent inhabitants of the province were too lazy to appropriate at their very doors."

Later on he went to Santa Barbara and in connection with his visit there relates the following interesting incident in regard to Ross. He says:

"Among the persons we met in Santa Barbara, was a lady of some historical celebrity. Von Resanoff, having failed, as elsewhere stated, in his attempt to enter the Columbia in 1806, continued his voyage as far as San Francisco, where, besides purchasing immediate supplies for Sitka, he endeavored, in negotiation with the commandant of the district and the governor of the province, to lay the foundation of a regular intercourse between Russian America and the Californian settlements. In order to cement the national union, he proposed uniting himself with Donna Conception Arguella, one of the commandant's daughters, his patriotism clearly being its own reward if half of Langsdorff's description was correct: 'She was lively and animated, had sparkling, love-inspiring eyes, beautiful teeth, pleasing and expressive features, a fine form, and a thousand other charms; yet her manners were perfectly simple and artless.'

"The chancellor, who was himself of the Greek Church, regarded the difference of religion with the eyes of a lover and a politician; but, as his imperial master might take a less liberal view of the matter, he posted away to St. Petersburgh with the intention, if he should there be successful, of subsequently visiting Madrid, for the requisite authority to carry his schemes into full effect. But the Fates, with a voice more powerful than that of emperors and kings, forbade the bans; and Von Resa-

noff died, on his road to Europe, at Krasnoyarsk in Siberia of a fall from his horse.

"Thus at once bereaved of her lover, and disappointed in her hope of becoming a pledge of friendship between Russia and Spain, Donna Conception assumed the habit, but not, I believe, the formal vows, of a nun, dedicating her life to the instruction of the young and the consolation of the sick. This little romance could not fail to interest us; and, notwithstanding the ungracefulness of her conventual costume and the ravages of an interval of time, which had tripled her years, we could still discover in her face and figure, in her manners and conversation, the remains of those charms which had won for the youthful beauty Von Resanoff's enthusiastic love and Langsdorff's equally enthusiastic admiration. Though Donna Conception apparently loved to dwell on the story of her blighted affections, yet, strange to say, she knew not, till we mentioned it to her, the immediate cause of the chancellor's sudden death. This circumstance might, in some measure, be explained by the fact, that Langsdorff's work was not published before 1814: but even then, in any other country than California, a lady, who was still young, would surely have seen a book, which, besides detailing the grand incident of her life, presented so gratifying a portrait of her charms."

We will close these extracts with the conclusion that the astute, if not brilliant, governor-general was forced to reach after he had fully felt the pulse of the situation in California.

He says:

"Now, for fostering and maturing Brother Jonathan's ambitious views, Captain Sutter's establishment is admirably situated. Besides lying on the direct route between San Francisco, on the one hand, and the Missouri and the Willamette, on the other, it virtually excludes the Californians from all the best parts of their own country, the valleys of the San Joaquin, the Sacramento, and the Colorado. Hitherto, the Spaniards have confined themselves to the comparatively barren strip of land, varying from ten to forty miles in width, which lies between the ocean and the first range of mountains; and beyond this slip they will never penetrate with their present character and their present force, if Captain Sutter, or any other adventurer, can gather round him a score of such marksmen as won Texas on the field of San Jacinto. But this is not all; for the Americans, if masters of the interior, will soon discover that they have a natural right to a maritime outlet; so that, whatever may be the fate of Monterey and the more southerly ports, San Francisco will, to a moral certainty, sooner or later, fall into the possession of Ameri-

cans—the only possible mode of preventing such a result being the previous occupation of the port on the part of Great Britain."

Sir George saw very clearly in the above forecast, for, six years after, the Americans took possession not only of the Fort of San Francisco but also of the entire province of California.

CHAPTER VIII.

The following account of a journey made by the distinguished Otto Von Kotzebue in 1824 from San Rafael to Ross by land cannot fail to interest. The journey was made in the beautiful month of September.

Captain Von Kotzebue was a sailor, a scientist and a man of acute sensibility—a splendid type of the aggressive Russian. One may read in this account between the lines a forecast of the ambition and love of country which since the time of the events described has so extended the territory, the wealth and the power of Russia.

It is also an interesting fact that Dr. Eschscholtz, for whom our State poppy flower was named, accompanied his chief on the journey. They had both been previously on the coast on a former voyage and had reached Ross from the sea side of the fort. On that voyage was Adelbert Von Chamisso, the botanist, and he had then given the name of his shipmate and friend, Dr. Eschscholtz, to this most brilliant and conspicuous of all the California flowers, which

prophetically uplifted a cup of gold to the future owners of California, which the Russians then hoped to be.

But that very year, though Von Kotzebue did not then know it, Minister Rush had concluded a treaty in London with Russia, under which Captain Von Kotzebue's imperial master had agreed to make no settlement on the northwest coast of America south of 54:40 north latitude. This was really the first step in the acquisition of California by the United States. It shut out all Russian pretensions, and Russia was the only country besides the United States which could quickly occupy the country by actual colonization.

With a word of encouragement from the home government all of California north of San Francisco would have been Russian long before 1846. The word never came. The treaty of 1824 had settled the question. But this was not known to Von Kotzebue, as, with his genial and brilliant conferee, Dr. Eschscholtz, he followed his guide Marco along the beautiful shore of the bay, speculating upon its value to his country, past the Olompali (now Burdell's station), up the San Antonio and through Two Rock valley to Bodega. The trail passed directly between the two split rocks which later on gave its name to the Two Rock country. What a splendid waste it was in those warm September days? The fat deer

moved reluctantly from their path. The elk were scattered like cattle over the hills. The coyote serenaded them at night, and the dreamy landscape, golden and green with grass and trees lay before the travelers just as it was shaped and colored by Nature's all-perfecting hand—well might it stir the sensitive heart and hand of a Von Kotzebue. His account of the land journey to Ross is as follows:

"Indispensable business now summoned me to the establishment of the Russian-American Company called Ross, which lies about eighty miles north of San Francisco. I had for some time been desirous of performing the journey by land, but the difficulties had appeared insurmountable. Without the assistance of the commandant, it certainly could not have been accomplished; I was therefore glad to avail myself of his friendly disposition towards me to make the attempt. We required a number of horses and a military escort; the latter to serve us at once as guides, and as a protection against the savages. Both these requests were immediately granted; and Don Estudillo himself offered to command the escort.

"My companions on this journey were Dr. Eschscholz, Mr. Hoffman, two of my officers, two sailors, Don Estudillo, and four dragoons, making altogether a party of twelve. On the evening previous to the day for our departure, Estudillo came to the ship with his four dragoons, the latter well armed, and accoutred in a panoply of leather. He himself, in the old Spanish costume, with a heavy sword, still heavier spurs, a dagger and pistols in his belt, and a staff in his hand, was a good personification of an adventurer of the olden time. He assured us that we could not be too cautious, since we should pass through a part of the country inhabited by "los Indianos bravos;" we therefore also made a plentiful provision of arms, and were ready, as soon as the first beams of morning glimmered on the tops of the mountains, to set forward in our barcasse for the mission of St. Rafael, lying on the northern shore of the bay, whence our land journey was to commence.

"The weather was beautiful, the wind perfectly still, and the air enchantingly mild. An Indian named Marco, whom Estudillo had with him, served us as a pilot; for the Spaniards here, incapable, either through indolence or ignorance, of discharging that office, always employ an experienced Indian at the helm.

"Don Estudillo, although advanced in life, was a very cheerful companion, and one of the most enlightened Spaniards I have met with in California. He piqued himself a little on his literary acquirements, and mentioned having read three books besides Don Quixote and Gil Blas, whilst, as he assured

me in confidence, the rest of his countrymen here had hardly ever seen any other book than the Bible. Marco had grown grey in the mission; on account of his usefulness, he had been in many respects better treated than most of the Indians: he spoke Spanish with tolerable fluency; and when Estudillo endeavored to exercise his wit upon him, often embarrassed him not a little by his repartees. This Marco affords a proof that, under favorable circumstances, the minds even of the Indians of California are susceptible of improvement; but these examples are rare in the missions.

"I confess I could not help speculating upon the benefit this country would derive from becoming a province of our powerful empire, and how useful it would prove to Russia. An inexhaustible granary for Kamtschatka, Ochotsk, and all the settlements of the American Company; these regions, so often afflicted with a scarcity of corn, would derive new life from a close connection with California.

The sun rose in full magnificence from behind the mountain, at the moment when, emerging from between the islands which divide the northern from the southern half of the bay, an extensive mirror of water opened upon our view. The mission of San Rafael, the first stage of our journey, formed a distinguished object in the background of the prospect, sloping up the sides of the hills, the intervening flat land lying so low that it was not yet within our horizon. We had also a distant view towards the northwest of another newly-founded mission, that of St. Francisco Salano (Sonoma), the only one situated on the northern shore of the bay except San Rafael.

"The country at this side of the bay, chiefly characterised by gently swelling hills, the park-like grouping of the trees, and the lively verdure of the meadows, is as agreeable to the eye as that of the southern coast. The water is pure and wholesome, which that at the Presidio is not; we therefore laid in our ship's store here.

"The whole Bay of St. Francisco, in which thousands of ships might lie at anchor, is formed by nature for an excellent harbor; but the little creeks about the northwest coast, now lying to our left, and which I have since frequently visited, are especially advantageous for repairs, being so deep that the largest vessels can lie conveniently close to the land; and an abundance of the finest wood for shipbuilding, even for the tallest masts, is found in the immediate neighborhood. The whole of the northern part of the bay, which does not properly belong to California, but is assigned by geographers to New Albion, has hitherto remained unvisited by voyagers, and little known even to the Spaniards residing in the country. Two large

navigable rivers, which I afterwards surveyed, empty themselves into it, one from the north, the other from the east. The land is extremely fruitful, and the climate is perhaps the finest and most healthy in the world. It has hitherto been the fate of these regions, like that o modest merit or humble virtue, to remain unnoticed; but posterity will do them justice; towns and cities will hereafter flourish where all is now desert; the waters, over which scarcely a solitary boat is yet seen to glide, will reflect the flags of all nations; and a happy, prosperous people receiving with thankfulness what prodigal Nature bestows for their use, will disperse her treasures over every part of the world.

" A fresh and favorable wind brought us, without much delay from the opposing ebb-tide, to the northern shore. We left the common embouchure of its two principal rivers, distinguished by the steepness of their banks to the right, and rowing up the narrow channel which has formed itself through the marsh land, reached our landing-place just as the sun's disk touched the summits of the mountains in the west.

CHAPTER IX.

"We were still distant a good nautical mile from the mission of St. Gabriel (Rafael), which peeped from amongst the foliage of its ancient oaks. Many horses belonging to the mission were grazing on a beautiful meadow by the waterside, in perfect harmony with a herd of small deer, which are very numerous in this country. Our dragoons, who had no inclination for a long walk, took their *lassos* in hand, and soon caught us as many horses as we wanted. We had brought our saddles with us, and a delightful gallop across the plain carried us to St. Rafael, where we we were received in a very hospitable manner by the only monk in residence.

"The locality of this mission, founded in 1816, is still better chosen than that of the celebrated Santa Clara. A mountain shelters it from the injurious north-wind; but the same mountain serves also as a hiding-place and bulwark for the *Indianos bravos*, who have already once succeeded in burning the buildings of the mission, and still keep the monks continually on the watch against similar depredations. In fact, St. Rafael has quite the appearance of an outpost for the defense of the other missions.

"The garrison, *six men* strong, is always ready for service on the slightest alarm. Having been driven from my bed at night by the vermin, I saw two sentinels, fully armed, keeping guard towards the mountain, each of them beside a large fire; every two minutes they rang a bell which was hung between two pillars, and were regularly answered by the howling of

Landing at Fort Ross as it is To-day

the little wolf I have before spoken of as often lurking in the vicinity of the missions. That there is not much to fear from other enemies, is sufficiently proved by the small number of soldiers kept, and the total neglect of all regular means of defense. The courage of these *bravos* seems indeed principally to consist in unwillingness to be caught, in flying with all speed to their hiding-places when pursued, and in setting fire to any property of the missions when they can find an opportunity of doing so unobserved. We saw here several of these heroes working patiently enough with irons on their feet, and in no way distinguishable in manners or appearance from their brethren of St. Francisco or Santa Clara.

"With the first rays of the sun we mounted our horses, and having passed the valley of St. Gabriel (Rafael), and the hill which bounds it, our guide led us in a north-westerly direction further into the interior. The fine, light, and fertile soil we rode upon was thickly covered with rich herbage, and the luxuriant trees stood in groups as picturesque as if they had been disposed by the hand of taste. We met with numerous herds of small deer, so fearless, that they suffered us to ride fairly into the midst of them, but then indeed darted away with the swiftness of an arrow. We sometimes also, but less frequently, saw another species of

stag, (elks) as large as a horse, with branching antlers; these generally graze on hills, from whence they can see round them on all sides, and appear much more cautious than the small ones. The Indians, however, have their contrivances to take them. They fasten a pair of the stag's antlers on their heads, and cover their bodies with his skin; then crawling on all-fours among the high grass, they imitate the movements of the creature while grazing; the herd, mistaking them for their fellows, suffer them to approach without suspicion, and are not aware of the treachery till the arrows of the disguised foes have thinned their number.

"Towards noon the heat became so oppressive, that we were obliged to halt on the summit of a hill: we reposed under the shade of some thick and spreading oaks, while our horses grazed and our meal was preparing. During our rest, we caught a glimpse of a troop of Indians skulking behind some bushes at a distance; our dragoons immediately seized their arms, but the savages disappeared without attempting to approach us. In a few hours we proceeded on our journey, through a country, which presenting no remarkable object to direct our course, excited my astonishment at the local memory of our guide, who had traversed it but once before. Two great shaggy white wolves, hunting a herd of

small deer, fled in terror on our appearance, and we had the gratification of saving the pretty animals for this time. In several places we saw little cylindrically-shaped huts of underwood, which appeared to have been recently quitted by Indians, and sometimes we even found the still glimmering embers of a fire; it is therefore probable that the savages were often close to us when we were not aware of it; but they always took care to conceal themselves from the much dreaded dragoons and their lassos.

"In the evening we reached a little mountain brook, which, after winding through a ravine, falls into the sea at Port Romanzow, or Bodega. It was already dark, and though but ten miles distance from Ross, we were obliged to pass the chill and foggy night not very agreeably on this spot. In the morning we forded the shallow stream, and as we proceeded, found in the bold, wild features of the scene a striking difference from the smiling valleys through which we had travelled on the preceding day. The nearer we drew to the coast, the more abrupt became the precipices and the higher the rocks, which were overgrown with larch even to their peaked summits.

"We wound round the bases of some hills, and having with much fatigue climbed other very steep ascents, reached towards noon a considerable height, which rewarded us with a magnificent prospect.

Amongst the remarkable objects before us, the ocean stretched to the west, with the harbor of Romanzow (Bodega), which unfortunately will only afford admission to small vessels; the Russian settlement here, can therefore never be as prosperous as it might have been, had circumstances permitted its establishment on the bay of St. Francisco. To the east, extending far inland, lay a valley, called by the Indians the Valley of the White Men (Santa Rosa). There is a tradition among them, that a ship was once wrecked on this coast; that the white men chose this valley for their residence, and lived there in great harmony with the Indians. What afterwards became of them is not recorded. On the northeast was a high mountain thickly covered with fir trees, from amongst which rose dark columns of smoke, giving evidence of Indian habitations. Our soldiers said that it was the abode of a chief and his tribe, whose valor had won the respect of the Spaniards; that they were of a distinct class from the common race of Indians; had fixed their dwellings on this mountain on account of its supposed inaccessibility; were distinguished for their courage, and preferred death to the dominion of the Missionaries, into whose power no one of them has ever yet been entrapped. Is it not possible that they may owe their superiority to having mingled their race with that of the shipwrecked whites?

"Our road now lay sometimes across hills and meadows, and sometimes along the sands so near the ocean that we were sprinkled by its spray. We passed Port Romanzow, and soon after forded the bed of another shallow river to which the Russians have given the name of Slavianka (Russian river). Farther inland it is said to be deeper, and even navigable for ships; its banks are extremely fertile, but peopled by numerous warlike hordes. It flows hither from the northeast; and the Russians have proceeded up it a distance of a hundred wersts, or about sixty-seven English miles.

"The region we now passed through was of a very romantic though wild character; and the luxuriant growth of the grass proved that the soil was rich. From the summit of a high hill, we at length, to our great joy, perceived beneath us the fortress of Ross, to which we descended by a tolerably convenient road. We spurred our tired horses, and excited no small astonishment as we passed through the gate at a gallop. M. Von Schmidt, the governor of the establishment, received us in the kindest manner, fired some guns to greet our arrival on Russian-American ground, and conducted us into his commodius and orderly mansion, built in the European fashion with thick beams.

"The settlement of Ross, situated on the seashore, in latitude 38° 33', and on an insignificant stream, was founded in the year 1812, with the free consent of the natives, who were very useful in furnishing materials for the buildings and even in their erection.

"The intention in forming this settlement was to pursue the chase of the sea-otter on the coast of California, where the animal was then numerous, as it had become extremely scarce in the more northern establishments. The Spaniards who did not hunt them, willingly took a small compensation for their acquiescence in the views of the Russians; and the sea-otter, though at present scarce even here, is more frequently caught along the California coast, southward from Ross, than in any other quarter. The fortress is a quadrangle, palisaded with tall, thick beams, and defended by two towers which mount fifteen cannons. The garrison consisted, on my arrival, of a hundred and thirty men, of whom a small number only were Russians, the rest Aleutians.

"The Spaniards lived at first on the best terms with the new settlers, and provided them with oxen, cows, horses and sheep; but when in process of time they began to remark that, notwithstanding the inferiority of soil and climate, the Russian establishment became more flourishing than theirs, envy and apprehension of future danger took possession of their minds; they then required that the settlement should be abandoned, — asserted

that their rights of domination extended northward quite to the Icy Sea, and threatened to support their claim by force of arms.

The founder and then commander of the fortress of Ross, a man of penetration, and one not easily frightened, gave a very decided answer. He had, he said, at the command of his superiors, settled in this region, which had not previously been in the possession of any other power, and over which, consequently, none had a right but the natives; that these latter had freely consented to his occupation of the land, and therefore that he would yield to no such unfounded pretension as that now advanced by the Spaniards, but should be always ready to resist force by force.

"Perceiving that the Russians would not comply with their absurd requisitions, and considering that they were likely to be worsted in an appeal to arms, the Spaniards quietly gave up all farther thought of hostilities, and entered again into friendly communications with our people; since which the greatest unity has subsisted between the two nations. The Spaniards often find Ross very serviceable to them. For, instance, there is no such thing as a smith in all California; consequently the making and repairing of all manner of iron implements here is a great accommodation to them, and affords lucrative employment to the Russians. The dragoons who accompanied us, had brought a number of old gunlocks to be repaired.

"In order that the Russians might not extend their dominion to the northern shore of the Bay of St. Francisco, the Spaniards immediately founded the missions of St. Gabriel (Rafael) and St. Francisco Salano (Sonoma). It is a great pity that we were not beforehand with them. The advantages of possessing this beautiful bay are incalculable, especially as we have no harbor but the bad one of Bodega or Port Romanzow.

"The inhabitants of Ross live in the greatest concord with the Indians, who repair, in considerable numbers, to the fortress, and work as day laborers for wages. At night they usually remain outside the palisades. They willingly give their daughters in marriage to Russians. and Aleutians; and from these unions ties of relationship have arisen which strengthen the good understanding between them. The inhabitants of Ross have often penetrated singly far into the interior, when engaged in the pursuit of deer or other game, and have passed whole nights among different Indian tribes, without ever having experienced any inconvenience. This the Spaniards dare not venture upon. The more striking the contrast between the two nations in their treatment of the savages, the more ardently must every friend to humanity rejoice on entering Russian territory.

" The climate at Ross is mild. Reaumur's thermometer seldom falls to the freezing point, yet gardens cannot flourish on account of the frequent fogs. Some wersts farther inland, beyond the injurious influence of the fog, plants of the warmest climates prosper surprisingly. Cucumbers of fifty pounds. weight, gourds of sixty-five, and other fruits in proportion, are produced in them. Potatoes yield a hundred or two hundred fold, and as they will produce two crops a year, are an effectual security against famine. The fortress is surrounded by wheat and barley fields, which, on account of the fogs, are less productive than those of Santa Clara, but which still supply sufficient corn for the inhabitants of Ross. The Aleutians find their abode here so agreeable, that although unwilling to leave their islands they are seldom inclined to return to them.

"The Spaniards should take a lesson in husbandry from M. Von Schmidt, who has brought it to an admirable degree of perfection. Implements, equal to the best we have in Europe, are made here under his direction. Our Spanish companions were struck with admiration at what he had done; but what astonished them most was the effect of a windmill; they had never before seen a machine so ingenious and so well adapted to the purpose.

" Ross is blest with an abundance of the finest wood for building.

The sea provides it with the most delicious fish, the land with an inexhaustible quantity of the best kinds of game; and, notwithstanding the want of a good harbor, the northern settlements might easily find in this a plentiful magazine for the supply of all their wants.

"The Indians of Ross are so much like those of the missions, that they may well be supposed to belong to the same race, however different their language. They appear indeed by no means stupid, and are much more cheerful and contented than at the missions, where a deep melancholy always clouds their faces, and their eyes are constantly fixed upon the ground; but this difference is only the natural result of the different treatment they experience. They have no permanent residence, but wander about naked, and, when not employed by the Russians as day laborers, follow no occupation but the chase. For the winter they lay up a provision of acorns and wild rye. The latter grows here very abundantly. When it is ripe they burn the straw away from it, and thus roast the corn, which is then raked together, mixed with acorns and eaten without any farther preparation. The Indians here have invented several games of chance. They are passionately fond of gaming, and often play away everything they possess. Should the blessing of civilization ever be extended to the rude inhab-

itants of these regions the merit will be due to the Russian settlements, certainly not to the Spanish missions.

"After a stay of two days we took leave of the estimable M. Von Schmidt and returned by the same way that we came without meeting with any remarkable occurrence. Professor Eschscholtz remained at Ross, in order to prosecute some botanical researches, intending to rejoin us by means of an Aleutian baidar, several of which were shortly to proceed to St. Francisco in search of otters.

"The Californian winter being now fairly set in we had much rain and frequent storms. On the 9th of October the southwest wind blew with the violence of the West-Indian tornado, rooted up the strongest trees, tore off the roofs of the houses, and occasioned great devastation in the cultivated lands. One of our thickest cables broke, and if the second had given way we would have been driven on the rocky shore of the channel which unites the bay with the sea, where a powerful current struggling with the tempest produced a frightful surf. Fortunately, the extreme violence of the storm lasted only a few hours, but in that short time it caused a destructive inundation: the water spread so rapidly over the low lands that our people had scarce time to secure the tent, with the astronomical apparatus.

"The arrival of Dr. Eschscholtz and the baidars from Ross was still delayed, and I really began to fear that some misfortune had befallen them in the tempest; my joy therefore was extreme when at last, on the 12th of October, the baidars, twenty in number, entered the harbor undamaged, and we received our friend again safe and well. The little flotilla had indeed left Ross before the commencement of the hurricane, but had fortunately escaped any injury from it, by taking refuge at a place called *Cap de los Regas*, till its fury was expended: but the voyagers had been obliged to bivouack on the naked rock, without shelter from the weather, and with very scanty provisions. Dr. Eschscholtz, however, not in the slightest degree disheartened by the difficulties he had undergone, was quite ready to join the voyage I had meditated for the examination of the adjacent rivers."

CHAPTER X.

The greatest difficulty the Russians had in maintaining their settlement in California was the absolute lack of interest the home government took in it. This was natural, as under the British treaty of 1824 made in London Russia had bound herself to make no settlement below 54° 40'.

The Russian-American Fur company, owing to its remoteness from the home government, was a sort of *imporium in imporio*. Its charter gave it governmental powers within

very limited restrictions. Alexander Baranoff, who ruled it so long with a rod of iron, used to say, "Heaven and the Czar are far off." The powers exercised by the Russian-American Fur Company were very despotic and had the force of imperial edicts within the jurisdiction of the company. It was a favorite idea with the Russian-American Company, originating with Baranoff, to get possession of

was an outgrowth of this desire. He used as an argument with the Californians for a concession of territory that the occupation of the northwest coast of California by the Russians would be a fence against the Americans, of whom the Californians had much dread, even at that early day. The Californians were, it is true, afraid of the Americans; but they were equally afraid of the Russians.

Fort Ross in 1830, looking South from the wharf

all California north of the bay and east of the Sacramento river for the purpose of raising and supplying grain to the fur hunters and Aleuts in the employ of the company on northwest coast.

This wish descended with the supreme control of affairs from Baranoff to his successors.

The expedition of baron Wrangel in 1830, heretofore referred to

They feared the Greek, though he came with gifts in his hand. In this they were wiser than the Chinese of the present day, who are granting concessions on their coast and privileges in their territory of Manchuria to the wily red-bearded man of the north, which they will find it difficult to recover if they hereafter wish to do so, for the Russian has never yet been dis-

placed where he once planted his aggressive foot and flag.

It was the intention of Baron Wrangel if he succeeded in attaining his object in Mexico to return to St. Petersburg with a concession of territory, which he hoped would cause his home government to take an interest in his scheme for the aggrandizement of his company and of his country by obtaining a foothold in California. The government at St. Petersburg only authorized him to negotiate a commercial treaty with Mexico so far as it related to its business on the Pacific coast, but nothing more. This scant authorization greatly embarrassed Wrangel on his arrival in Mexico. His principal aim was to get permission to colonize the north-west coast of California, but his power was limited to the negotiation of a commercial treaty.

When the Mexican government had fully sounded the authority of Baron Wrangel it very properly declined any further discussion of the matter with one who bore such limited credentials. All he could do was to get an assurance that Mexico would favor a commercial treaty if properly negotiated between accredited agents of the two governments. And declining further negotiation referred the subject to the Mexican minister at London, who was instructed to consider any proposition that might be made by his Imperial Majesty, the Emperor of all the Russians,

for the privileges asked by Baron Wrangel. No proposition was made of course. The St. Petersburg government took no step in the matter, well knowing that it was bound hand and foot so far as the acquisition of country in California went by its treaty stipulation with the United States.

One effect of the movement of Baron Wrangel was that it called the attention of the central government in Mexico, and the home colonial government in California, to the importance of North California, and pending the negotiations between 1831-6, orders were issued for the establishment of a presidio in the town of Sonoma, which was done in 1833 under the direction of General Vallejo, who was made commandant of the frontier.

The new commander was instructed to prevent any further encroachments upon Mexican territory by the Russians. With this view he established Black McIntosh and Dawson next to the Russian farm, in Bodega, and between 1833-9 all the best lands in what is now Sonoma county was granted to Mexican citizens.

By this time fur hunting had become less profitable on the coast of California, and the otter was about exterminated in the bay of San Francisco.

The hope of acquiring territory having failed with the failure of Wrangel's mission to Mexico, it

was determined by the Russian American Company to abandon Ross. This conclusion must have been a relief to the home government who had acquiesced in the occupation of Ross but had never made any claim of sovereignty, or attempt to acquire it, over the land.

Alexander Rotcheff, the last Russian governor, in connection with Kostromitinoff, a special agent of the company, under instructions from the directors, commenced negotiations in 1839 for the sale of the building, stock and mobilier of Ross. They first tried to sell it to the Hudson Bay Company, but this company did not want to buy. They next proposed to General Vallejo to sell it to the Mexican government. This proposal General Vallejo rejected with scorn, because, as he wrote to Governor Alvarado, "these buildings were built on Mexican soil with material from the same land, and belonged of right to the government, and, he adds, 'yes, most excellent senor; soon will the national flag wave gloriously and triumphantly where was hoisted a foreign flag during five lustres; the imperial eagles will yield the field to the eagle of Mexico, which we shall see for the first time soaring and spreading his protecting wings over this portion of our glorious country—lopped off from the mother land by the fur-hunting Russians'"

While the hauty Castilian General Vallejo was so gaily sporting the Mexican eagle from the flag-staff of Ross in his vivid imagination, the shrewd Rotcheff was negotiating with Captain Sutter for the purchase of the fort, and it soon after passed into his hands, to the great indignation of the Commandate del Fronteria, who always contended that the Russians had nothing to sell and Sutter had acquired nothing from them. This belief he would have enforced at the point of Mexican lances if he had had the lances and the lancers to bear them. It was not from a lack of courage that he let Sutter take possession but because he could not help it.

The Russians were now on the eve of their departure for California. They had begun their long journey toward it in the latter part of the century when Yermac, the Cossack robber, crossed the Ural mountains with his band of marauders, which ended with conquest of Siberia. As early as 1730 the Russians had reached the Pacific Ocean, colonizing the intervening six thousand miles of country, and in 1740 they crossed over Behring straits to the American continent and by the close of that century they had solidly established themselves on the northwest coast of America. They did not stop there but pushed down the coast, reaping a rich harvest of furs as they went, and finally, as has heretofore been told, took possession of Bodega Bay in 1812, which they held until 1840.

Strangely enough in this last year Wossnessensky, a naturalist attached to the zoological museum of St. Petersburg, arrived at Ross. He had been sent to the coast of eastern Asia and northwest America by the Academy of Science and had been making collections on the Asiatic and American seashore.

From the mountain back of Ross which rises to a great height, a beautiful view of St. Helena mountain may be seen to the eastward. Its elevation above the sea level is 4,343 feet, and it is the most conspicuous feature in the landscape of the four counties of Sonoma, Napa, Marin and Lake. It can be seen from far out at sea and also from the city of San Francisco. Wossnessensky doubtless saw it looming up in all its stately grandeur from the Ross Ridge. To so adventurous a spirit as his, to see was to visit it; to visit it was to determine to ascend it. This he did on June 12, 1841 He named it St. Helena in honor of his imperial mistress the Empress of Russia and, planting a post on its highest point, he nailed to it a copper plate inscribed with the name he had given the mountain, his own name and that of his companion (Tscherneeh) with the date of the ascent and the word "Russians" twice repeated, once in Russian, once in Latin. The mountain has ever since retained the name given to it in this notable christening, and will stand forever as an enduring monument of the most easterly and most southerly point touched by the Russians in their advance across Siberia and the Pacific Ocean to northwest America, and thence down the coast to California.

The Russians retired from California, and later on from Alaska because, south of Siberia, there was a richer and even greater field for their aggressive ambition; and today that mighty empire holds the destiny not alone of Asia but of Europe in the hollow of its potential hand.

*9 7 8 3 3 3 7 1 6 9 5 1 0 *